Liturgy and Urban Mission

Tim Stratford

Vicar, Church of the Good Shepherd,
West Derby, Liverpool

GROVE BOOKS LIMITED
RIDLEY HALL RD CAMBRIDGE CB3 9HU

Contents

I am most grateful to the people of the Good Shepherd, West Derby for their tolerance and willingness to explore new avenues. May I also add my thanks to members of GROW who have encouraged me to write this booklet and especially to Anne Hollinghurst and Ian Tarrant who have helped with the text. I do not pretend that it is the last word in urban liturgical thinking but I hope it is a useful contribution.

The Cover Illustration is by Peter Ashton

First Impression December 2002
ISSN 0144-1728
ISBN 1 85174 516 5

Introduction 1

The chapters that follow are written out of my experience of being Vicar on a large Liverpool outer urban estate.

It has many things in common with other Urban Priority Areas (UPAs) but also has its own distinctive features. For example, only 0.9% of people here are from ethnic minorities and only 0.3% of people describe themselves as black. But there is much that is shared between UPAs, and it may help if I define some common (and overlapping) terms which I will use later:

- *UPA:* I use this with the same sense it has in *Faith in the City*.[1] UPAs are usually determined as being places where a high percentage of people have a low income. The Church of England considers parishes as UPAs where the Oxford Low Income Predictor (based on Census data) suggests 17% or more of households to have a low income.

- *Area of Multiple Deprivation:* This term does not involve a moral judgment but refers to areas where many of the things that enhance life, taken for granted across most of Britain, are missing. AMDs tend to be recognized through analysis of whole community characteristics rather than the personal and individual responses collected by the census. For example, the DETR Index of Deprivation uses health service, education and geographic data such as proximity of local services to form a ranking table of deprived electoral wards. Many rural areas are high in the index.

- *Working Class:* This does not refer to a locality but to the cultural identity that people have. It is not a precise term, nor does it belong to a monochrome and homogeneous group, but it does serve as a useful label. It describes characteristics that large numbers of people share together as a result of their history and background.

The experience of worship in a UPA church can sometimes seem very inadequate compared with the beauty and vibrancy that fills other places. But our quest is not simply for 'glorious' or 'perfect' worship—more for 'real' worship. I hope that what follows is real and can helpfully illumine your own worship.

2   Theological Background

'Urban' is a very misused word. It conjures up images of grey tower blocks, broken streets, crime, violence, low educational standards, poor health, unemployment and angry youths.

But in Britain some of our most prosperous communities are urban, as are many historical landmarks such as cathedrals and palaces. If we can judge popularity by where most people spend most of their time then we must conclude that human beings like urban centres. Since the early nineteenth century more than half of the people of Britain have lived in urban communities and at the start of the twenty-first century the figure is 80%.[2] Many residential urban communities are spacious and green places to live. You are more likely to find excellent communications and transport systems, comprehensive provision of public service, commerce and leisure facilities in urban communities than in the countryside. But still the term 'urban' conveys a sense of bleakness.

Of course, not all people who live in urban places share the benefits equally. Huge areas of cities and towns, especially the outer urban estates, are characterized by severe deprivation. This is indicated by factors such as low income, high unemployment, low academic achievement, high morbidity rates and poor quality housing. These things contribute to an oppression of the human spirit and the community spirit that in turn becomes part of a cycle, making things worse. So they are spiritual issues that are characterized by low horizons and self-esteem, a lack of beauty and things that stimulate the aesthetic senses, little hope and a sense of being on the edge. In the 1980s the Archbishop of Canterbury's Commission adopted the term 'Urban Priority Areas' or 'UPAs' and brought it into widespread use across the church. The terms 'UPA' and 'urban' are not synonymous but if there is to be any sense of 'priority' about areas of multiple deprivation then it may not be surprising that their needs dominate urban thinking.

If the Church of England's strength in mission can be discerned by where it is able to gather the most worshippers then it has clearly been amongst the middle classes. Ted Wickham, in his important book, *Church and People in an Industrial City*,[3] charted some of the reasons why he believed rural workers migrating to towns and cities during the Industrial Revolution never reconnected with church worship. Along with the consequences of dislocation were issues such as underprovision of churches in the city areas they moved into and no place for them in the churches that did exist, compounded by the pew rent system. It may be that his estimation of the number of rural workers who had connected with the eighteenth century Church of England in the countryside was coloured by more than a little optimistic romanticism. Nevertheless, he puts his finger on important evidence to show that the church was simply ill-equipped and unprepared to find a place for the urban working classes.

In his preface to the publication of the 1851 Religious Census data, the statistician Horace Mann stated:

> ...it must be apparent that a sadly formidable portion of the English people are habitual neglecters of the public ordinances of religion...The masses of our working population...are never or but seldom seen in our religious congregations.[4]

At the time this forged a new resolve in the Church of England. Churches were built. Dioceses were created. Pew rents were abolished. But there still remained something intangibly middle class about it all.

The Slum-Priest-Ritualists have passed into the mythology of the Church of England as examples of those who offered the possibility of a culture change. They were formed in the light of the spiritual awakening of the Oxford Movement in the first half of the nineteenth century and practised as priests in the latter half. Their concerns were expressed liturgically and it was over worship that they had their greatest battles. They were amongst the minority of Anglican clergy who were prepared to pay the personal price of working in poor communities. The churches being built in the slums, with no long-established tradition, were a magnet to these characters who wanted to do something new. In time, some of these priests did grow churches where the urban poor found for themselves a spiritual home. For a short time they also rode on a wave of popularity that drew its energy from the oppression they suffered at the hands of the hierarchy. From amongst their number there were early deaths, long-running battles with bishops through the ecclesiastical courts and imprisonments. It may be that the urban poor truly identified with these things and saw in them something of the gospel being reflected. Although some of their liturgical practices seeped into the wider church these were the mere mechanics. The more painful questions they provoke of what it means to identify in worship with the experience of living in urban priority areas, such as where the Church stands in relation to power, still rarely trouble the conscience of much of the Church of England even today.

UPA Culture

It is probably not possible to set out a single definitive description of either middle class or working class British culture but there are some broad values that can be used to help make a distinction. Whilst this does not define, it does serve to illustrate matters. It is also possible to see some of the historical roots out of which these values have grown and so understand why it is legitimate to talk in general terms of working class culture and middle class culture. The purpose of this is not to pigeonhole people but to understand communities and how it is that the church can be perceived as belonging to 'us' or belonging to 'them.'

There are four key areas of difference: language, education, money and identity. I will outline these below, and explore them further in the chapters that follow. There is a fifth vital issue, that of self-esteem, which I will address in the final chapter.

Language

B Bernstein has demonstrated that language is used quite differently in working class and middle class cultures.[5] There is some debate about whether the differences he observes can be as mechanistically associated with particular aspects of middle class or working class life as he suggests, but his observations of difference remain valid. The notions of a restricted code characterizing working class speech and an elaborate code characterizing middle class speech are at the heart of his work. It is not contentious to state that we learn how to use language according to our need to communicate with others around us and the modes by which they communicate with us. Language is shaped by culture and in turn contributes to that culture's propagation.

> *Language is used quite differently in working class and middle class cultures*

Speech that conforms to an elaborate code uses an extensive vocabulary and a precise agreement about the meanings of words to communicate successfully. So, for instance, a wholehearted reply to a question about going out to the cinema might run along the lines of, 'Yes. I'd really love to go. I've been wanting to see that film for weeks and a night out with you would be great!'

Speech that uses a restricted code tends to rely more heavily on intonation and body language to communicate subtlety rather than a large vocabulary of descriptive words and sub-clauses. So, in parts of Liverpool the word 'yeah' alone can mean anything from 'no, not really' to the positive fulsome reply of the paragraph above, depending on context and how it is said.

Restricted code speech tends to be very locally based. For those who come into such communities from outside it can be very difficult to understand. Elaborate code speech has the capacity for its rules to be more universally shared and widely understood. Middle class English is a prime example of where this has happened. This is inevitably the means by which language is used in writing and the mass media. Indeed its speakers believe their use of language is almost universal. Those who have grown up in working class communities can find themselves tongue-tied and unable to communicate properly in middle class contexts. If they want to live in this bigger world they have to learn how to talk all over again.

In the church, shared words are central and an elaborate speech code dominates

A church that wants to represent the gospel in UPAs needs to give time to learn how language works there and needs to have the flexibility to adapt. The arrogance which says that the locals need to learn to speak English 'properly' fails to recognize that there is more than one legitimate way of speaking and handicaps the church's mission. This is a real challenge to the liturgical enterprise of the church, where shared words are central and an elaborate speech code dominates.

Education

In middle class communities, education tends to be regarded as of high value and a human right. In working class communities it is more likely to be regarded as something done to children until they are old enough to move on. This is not surprising. One culture has been formed by society's valuing the creative work of the mind whilst the other has been formed by society's valuing the work of the hands. Education, as distinct from training, has as its goal the stimulation of the mind. Whilst this may have benefit to everybody it does not have the same sort of value within a working class culture as does training in a skill.

Undoubtedly the boundary between education and training, general and vocational learning, is blurring. And in working class communities there is a growing recognition that education is increasingly important in equipping people for the work place. But this varies across the generations and older generations influence the young more than the young influence the old.

Perceptions of education will clearly affect the ways that communities respond to the church. There has been a strong tendency in preparation for Church of England ministry to focus on education. Skills are often undervalued. A natural pastor may still need to obtain a degree before being ordained whereas a professor of theology is likely to be ordained whether or not they have a pastoral bone in their body.

Money

Very rarely will you find a bank on outer urban estates or in the midst of poor inner city communities. The middle classes cannot transact their business without such facilities and are increasingly marginalizing those communities that have never had access to finance. The roots of the current situation in history are plain. Middle classes have tended to be monthly salaried and paid directly into a bank account held in their name. The British working classes have traditionally been weekly paid in cash or, for casual labour, even paid daily at an hourly rate in cash. The middle classes have needed to budget and have developed a culture that can cope with mortgage loans several times larger than a year's income. In working class communities, loans can be terrifying. The weekly pay packet encouraged weekends of plenty and days of scarcity. Similarly, bills are paid weekly by means of TV licence stamps, pre-payment gas and electricity meters. Conventional wisdom encourages the view that what people cannot pay for they do not buy. Credit is called the 'never never.'

The capacity to celebrate and commiserate is far more alive

Frugality is a middle class value. In working class culture bounty and dearth are part of the inevitable shape of life. These things betray a sense of humanity in working class culture that can often be missing in middle class communities. The capacity to celebrate and commiserate is far more alive. In working class communities the occasional offices are much more likely to have significance right across the community, whereas elsewhere their significance is likely to be restricted to a particular family.

Identity

The middle classes are increasingly equipped to be highly mobile and there is an expectation in many work places and amongst employers that people are prepared to move about. The decision to move is normally based on what is best for a relatively small circle of people, often an individual. New private owner-occupier housing estates are likely to offer a great deal of privacy from neighbours. This helps sell houses but in the longer term turns into what has been described as 'designer isolation.'

Many working class families have grown up in houses that were too small for them. Members of the extended family lived near by. The street was an extension of the home. It then becomes natural to think corporately. In some Liverpool communities the word 'us' is often substituted where others might say 'I.'

It is easy to be romantic about this. Undoubtedly some of the strongest features of the corporate nature of working class communities are breaking down. Availability of housing, dependence on the motorcar and employers' expectations may well be part of the reason for this. Despite this, there is still a strong sense of the value of corporate identity that tends to distinguish this cultural self-understanding from the individualism of the middle classes.

There is great potential resonance here with *koinonia* within the traditions of the church, and there may need to be some re-learning of the nature of a gospel that has often been individualized, especially amongst evangelicals.

There is great potential resonance here with koinonia within the traditions of the church

Accepting Cultural Difference

Prejudice is something that seems to belong to all cultures. The middle classes are likely to argue that working class cultures do not exist and to regard people formed by such backgrounds as simply impoverished potential middle class people. Working class communities are likely to write off middle class institutions as not belonging to 'us' and write off middle class individuals as untrustworthy. Yet somehow the gospel of Christ calls the church to be more inclusive than that.

There is not space here to dwell on the earliest struggles of the church to come to terms with the difference between Jewish Christian and Gentile Christian ways as betrayed by Acts 15 and Galatians 2. And it may be that the church has never really managed to achieve what was clearly an ideal drawn from the heart of all that Jesus stood for. The disciples themselves were a mismatched and diverse group; Jesus taught love of neighbour, welcomed Roman soldiers into the kingdom and imagined a Good Samaritan. Whilst power in today's Church of England is in the hands of the more eloquent, more ideas-focused, more prosperous and more individualistic middle classes, there remains a vital mission imperative to those who have been kept on the edge for too long. The church must respond to this by re-inventing itself in cultural terms other than those with which it has been most comfortable.

3

There is an inevitability about the fact that middle class English dominates the Church of England's central structures and, consequently, its official liturgies.

It would not be reasonable to expect the church to develop texts that conform to local usages of language but it perhaps ought to recognize that such usages are a reality.

How Does God Communicate With Us?

God's word cannot be confined to certain linguistic modes. Some people might argue that it can only be discerned reliably through the pages of the Bible. Others could argue the same through the worship texts of the church. But there are many other ways by which God's ways are communicated to us, for example:

- Creation speaks, or as Psalm 65 says, 'the gates of the morning and evening sing your praise.'
- Music, art and the aesthetic stir the spirit.
- The examples of the saints (great and small) inspire.
- The life of Christ is mediated by story that transcends sentence structure and vocabulary.
- The compassion and support of faithful brothers and sisters encourages.
- In the quiet of our own hearts, God's still small voice speaks to our minds and informs our consciences.

Agrarian and Urban Imagery

When language is used figuratively it can conjure up a set of mental pictures that say more than the words can themselves. When we are talking about the things of eternity we often have to resort to the use of metaphor and simile because plain language is too temporal. Jesus' teaching often begins, 'The kingdom of heaven is like…' He would then choose similes from within the experience of those he spoke to—a mustard seed, a farmer, an estate manager, and so on. His teaching was not exclusively rural but it is these agrarian images that have stayed best with the Church of England. A 'town built upon a hill cannot be hidden' is less firmly rooted in the consciousness.

The Bible was formed in an age and place that was dominated by agrarian concerns and inevitably that shapes the church's repertoire of imagery. This is reflected in the official liturgical resources of the church but is just as great an issue in the culture of jargon that is used almost unconsciously. This includes preaching, hymnody and song.

These images from a distant way of life can become comfortable retreats for cosy religious gatherings. This was never how they were intended. Indeed, they made such strong connections for people that faith was challenged and shaken by Jesus. There must be experiences of urban living that resonate with the eternal dimension and shed light on God's kingdom in lively ways today. Some church groups, such as the Iona Community, are extending our vocabulary but their impact in many churches is yet to be felt.

Literacy

We discussed above some issues that revolve around education for people who live in working class communities. Cultural responses to academic learning are some of the root causes of low attainment and contribute to the levels of deprivation that afflict some places. Associated with all of this are very low levels of literacy. This can add to the sense of alienation that people can feel with a church when worship revolves around printed words.

But alongside this must be set the experience of local people who have come to comprise the church in a UPA. Many of them may well have found personal growth in publicly reading the Bible or leading intercessions. And they will have made these steps without necessarily having developed the same sorts of reading skills as many middle class people will have. There is a real challenge for UPA churches in giving their members the opportunity to grow as co-leaders of the worship. Should people who find reading hard be encouraged into roles that require this as a skill or are there ways of leading worship that do not rely on reading?

The easy way out is clericalism. UPA clergy may find that they can lead every aspect of worship in more refined ways than members of their congregation. But those who choose to do so will find they are holding back the mission of the church. The participation of local people in leadership helps proclaim the message that the worship of God is the work of all the people. It does not belong to the professionals but to the church. It needs to be done. And it needs to be done right, not just following the models of every member ministry as they have been developed in other conventional contexts.

Moreover, if it is difficult for people to break into the leadership of worship because of reliance on the printed word it may also be difficult for people simply to worship. *Common Worship* has not improved the situation. For instance, many of the responses to Eucharistic Prayers require the worshipper to follow the text closely; triggers for responses are not predicable unless people have learnt the whole prayer; responses vary from paragraph to paragraph within the same prayer. Texts need to have a simpler rhythm in parishes where following the printed word is not a straightforward matter.

Rote and Familiarity

Any regular communion visitor to a nursing home cannot help but notice how some familiar prayers can trip off the tongue of people who find even conversation difficult. You only need to say, 'Our Father,' and you can attract rapt attention. Familiar prayers, once learnt by rote, are a key spiritual resource where printed prayers are not helpful.

Common Worship allows for change in the basic ingredients of worship week after week. To some extent this might be a reaction against the fixed and stultified worship that the *Book of Common Prayer* sometimes engendered. But worship patterns that change week in and week out will not help people commit a great deal to memory. And in communities where liturgical memory is as important as the printed word this can most definitely get in the way.

This is not an argument for stultifying *Common Worship* but it does demonstrate the need for careful consideration of the use of orders of service. Whilst a new order of service every week might be too much to take, a fresh liturgy for each season of the church's year (nine changes per annum) can be both manageable and helpful. Resources such as Susan Sayers' *Prayers through the Year* or *Living Stones* tend to encourage alternative forms of intercession with different responses each week. In some communities it may be too much even to do this. Try varying the outline for intercessions on a seasonal basis too. Remember that ASB Rite A only encouraged the one form of intercessions for use year in and year out.

Repeats

Within a single act of worship people can be made slaves to the printed word if they are expected to respond in unison to the liturgy in a variety of different and unexpected ways. This is not to say that the vocal response of a congregation to prayer is undesirable, far from it, but not every response needs to be unique. Beware of the overuse of Eucharistic Prayers that adopt this device in particular. Confessions where the words of the people are simply *kyries* or liturgies such as 'The Litany' may offer better models.

Rhythm and Rhyme

A third device with historical credibility is the use of rhythm and rhyme. Most of us learnt the alphabet or our 'times tables' as children in this way. Some *Common Worship* texts such as Eucharistic Prayer D pick this up. An Affirmation of Faith such as that found on page 146 of *Common Worship* also works with music. Whilst it does not have the orthodox credentials of the Nicene Creed it may be much easier for people to commit to memory.

Communicating in Other Ways

Language extends beyond the spoken word. We can communicate much through our body language. The worlds of, for instance, the artist, the iconographer, the dancer, the musician and the dramatist, also have a language all of their own. And we do not necessarily need to be initiated into the technicalities of those languages for these things to mediate eternal truths to us. Although a high level of skill may be necessary before these modes are at their best, this does not inhibit their use in UPA churches. Visual and dramatic skills are certainly more finely honed in some of Liverpool's UPAs than are those that are more cerebral or academic.

The Evangelical tradition, in particular, has tended to shun the visual, aesthetic and emotionally evocative in worship. So churches tend to be plain, art is minimalist and the liturgy limited in drama. The arts can be seen as cloaking the truth. This has strength in the way that the tradition has been able to help people focus on the simplest elements of a faith bound in the historical truth of the Bible. But in communities where plain words are not enough then visual, dramatic and musical interpretation can demystify. This can include:

- Clipart as visual cues on the service sheet;
- Photos and moving images on a PowerPoint presentation or OHP;
- Work from the children's groups being displayed around the walls;
- Artwork from a local iconographer on easels in the chancel;
- Congregational action during prayer and worship;
- Dance and drama;
- Symbols, both new and traditional.

4   Praxis (the Practical Side)

It is in the nature of the Church of England that the majority of its professional clergy are middle class.

And those of us who were not middle class before training for ordination will undoubtedly be more so afterwards. This is a self-propagating cycle. Ordained Local Ministry (OLM) has been promoted as a means to break the cycle. The local congregation have responsibility for discerning somebody's call and the local context is taken into account in the selection process. But even here the culturally-biased measures used for other clergy can filter out those who have not been formed in a middle class way.

In turn, the clergy help define the leadership of a local church

In turn, the clergy help define the leadership of a local church. Those who find themselves with responsibilities in a parish will most often be those who have learnt how to work alongside the clergy.

In working class communities this can lead to a culture clash between a church's leadership and the way that the community most naturally operates.

Planning and Short-termism

In the parish in which I work, the Good Shepherd, West Derby (Liverpool), only the parish staff, Churchwardens and Treasurer have diaries. People are well able to remember complex patterns of dates for events and meetings but it is not done by resort to paper. There is a finely-tuned corporate memory that is able to alert people to a commitment they have a day or two beforehand. Hospital appointments and anniversaries do tend to get recorded on a calendar in the living room but church dates rarely get recorded here. The community remembers for people.

Of course, planning for worship is done on paper. But if rotas, lectionaries and service details remain on paper they will not happen. Papers, notice sheets and magazines are not routinely referred to. Somehow these things have to be transferred into the local corporate memory. And it is immensely frustrating when you discover only two days before a major festival service that the people who were due to contribute to it are going away on holiday.

The more that leaders try to organize these frustrations out the more frustrating they will become. A truly indigenous church would not even try to organize something until the week before it is due to happen. Clergy need to walk a difficult boundary between wanting their own working patterns organized enough to be able to operate well, but being in a community that lives on a day-by-day basis. This can seem on the one side as if local people are unreliable and on the other side as if church leaders are too managerial. It may be necessary to work out those things which simply must be worked out well in advance but then to relax about the details that people simply will not take an interest in until nearer the time. And the more predictable the pattern that the long term planning has, the better. Patterns lodge better in the memory than isolated and individual dates.

The more predictable the pattern that the long term planning has, the better

Leading Worship

Communities whose members have been excluded from many leading roles in society are bound to be cynical of those who seek to exercise authority over them. Urban Priority Areas tend to have very few captains of industry or 'bosses' living in them. Those who seek to offer leadership within UPA churches as 'boss' are likely to be faced with more cynicism than obedience. In these communities leadership is an honour that must be earned.

The way that worship is led can be read as symbolic of how ministers see themselves in relation to those around them. In working class cultures relational messages can be read very quickly and easily. Those who lead worship as a messiah with all the answers will be seen through very quickly indeed. Those whose trust is more in their own judgment than in the wisdom of the community that surrounds them are likely to be perceived as foreigners out of touch with how things happen 'round here.'

So some of the dos and don'ts of leading worship begin to become clear:

DO	• Be humble and act humbly • Share leadership of worship with others • Listen and evaluate alongside others • Earn the right to be trusted
DON'T	• See yourself as a saviour • Be authoritarian • Assume you have the right to lead before you have earned it

Preaching

Being able to listen to the local community is always needed to draw people into the worship of God. But it is even more important when opening the Word of God up for reflection and learning. Whereas in middle class churches people might be drawn to the 'teaching,' in working class communities they could all too easily be alienated by it. Those of us who have an understanding that has been formed by academia of how the Bible and faith combine to change lives, and who have middle class assumptions, will seem to be very remote to the immediacy of most UPA contexts.

There are undoubtedly members of UPA churches whose lives have been changed by the church's bashing out of its conventional wisdom. But on the whole many more are mystified. The stories, sketches, poems and resonances that illustrate sermons in middle England might have no connection at all with those who live on society's edges. This is possibly why a more searching and questioning model of preaching is being adopted in these places. Sermons that open up the Bible enough for its joys and struggles to become visible and which then openly ask, 'So what does that mean in this place and at this time?' can be renewing and revitalizing for the church.[6] It is important to give time then for the question to be addressed by the congregation. This way illustration is provided that is not concocted at the study desk but that has been lived locally. Those who lead and preach are also delivered from the pressure of being the focus of all the answers and are placed in a more humble and listening role in relation to the worshipping community.

This way illustration is provided that is not concocted at the study desk but that has been lived locally

There are, of course, other models of preaching in UPA churches that have validity. Whatever model is used it will always be important that the minister is rooted and grounded amongst the concerns of their community rather than dropping down instructions from elsewhere.

Sharing Leadership

Sharing the leadership of worship is not always easy in places where multiple deprivation across generations has led to a community with low self-esteem and low levels, or even the complete absence, of some skills in the areas of music and literacy. But people's relational skills in working class cultures are often very much higher than they are in other places. And authentic local leadership, especially of worship, is vital to the mission of the church in communities that have felt estranged from it.

It may well be that for some people the leadership of regularly repeated phrases from the liturgy is easier than reading from Exodus or leading intercessions. Perhaps our models for leading Communion should extend beyond the conventions of a president and deacon.

Teams can be trained to pray quietly with individuals during services of Wholeness and Healing or for administering Communion. Working with teams, and the corporate learning that can go along with this, is much more natural in many working class communities than individually going on a course would be. The Liverpool Diocese has run training schemes for UPA parishes since 1985 that capitalize on the strength of group work in working class cultures.[7] But do not assume the local church will necessarily have confidence in a hand-picked group. Make sure that consultation and selection are done in a broad-based way.

Leadership is not just focussed in the carrying out of a function but is also exercised in the planning for and evaluation of events. Worship Committees can be helpful in encouraging this to happen in a way that enables things to be seen through local cultural filters. It is important that such groups give good time to offer real critical evaluation, especially where something new has been tried out. It is also important that they give things a chance to settle and are wise enough not simply to jump on or off bandwagons. Before they even begin their work they should take time to think through what worship is about and especially to realize that what the church is about is not 'perfect worship' but 'real worship.' The two may be quite different things. In creating such groups try to ensure that most perspectives within the church's community are represented or understood somehow.

Music

Music is an essential dimension of worship and can be greatly enriching—but is a real challenge for some UPA churches. Congregations can be small, the skill base low, and expectations limited by the memories of the organ when it worked properly. These are problems that affect churches further afield too. Many UPA churches have been leading the way forward with solutions that are sometimes innovative and sometimes obvious:

- *Iona:* The Wild Goose Worship Group and members of the Iona Community from inner city Glasgow have produced a large amount of song, hymnody and liturgical music that can be sung unaccompanied or with very simple accompaniment. Much of it makes very strong connections with the challenges of faith in poor urban contexts. Some of this is also available on tape or CD, which provides a means of learning it.

- *Music-go-round:* In a neighbourhood or deanery where the skills of individual churches are small it may be that collectively a group could come together for support and inspiration. Such groups can become the way by which new music is discovered and learnt locally. They can also do a round Sunday by Sunday providing accompaniment and teaching new songs in churches on a rotational basis.

- *Midi:* Music recorded as a midi data file is not like a conventional sound recording. These files can only be played back through an instrument. They contain no sounds but only the notation, timing and control instructions that would otherwise have been supplied by a musician playing the instrument. They can be used in many keyboards and can be played through plug-in boxes on most electronic church organs. Where organists are in high demand a church can borrow somebody from another church in the middle of the week. They can combine a practice of Sunday's music whilst also recording midi files for playback on Sunday. The files can be kept on a computer from which disks can also be created for other occasions. There are also a number of small, dedicated midi data players that will feed a church sound system with easily selected accompaniment for hymns and songs from commercially available CDs.[8]

- *Providing lessons for people:* Churches are the places in UPAs where people are most often inspired to lift their horizons and believe that 'I could do that.' Keyboard, woodwind and guitar lessons are often available to people in areas of multiple deprivation free. Or it may be possible for the local church to subsidise somebody and inspire him or her to learn an instrument. The benefits can be felt quite quickly by the church and are huge to the individual.

- *Background music:* Remember that music is not just an item punctuating a service for which people must stand and sing. You can, for instance, use simple chants such as Taizé under spoken prayer or play carefully chosen music from a CD during quiet reflection, or when people are receiving Communion or before and after worship.

- *Music from beyond the church:* A great deal of contemporary music deals with questions of who we are, where we stand in relation to others, yearnings of the heart and love. Many people will find themselves identifying with them quite easily and some will be able to sing them more easily than hymns. They can simply be played for reflection from original recordings. This is an increasingly common element in funeral services. For other occasions accompaniment and words can be found on karaoke CDs and for many there is sheet music available.

- *Choruses and simple songs:* The complexities of faith are always important and in communities were life is hard this is most obvious to people. Worship songs can sometimes gloss over things that are difficult. Choose simple songs carefully and watch the theology.

Being Immediate in Prayer

The practice of worship always being staged and led from the front is a formality that UPA congregations have not been slow to challenge. Answering back during the sermon is one example. Chipping in with immediate issues for prayer is another. There is no reason why such requests cannot be canvassed before intercessions are led or by means of a book people can write in on their way into church. Sometimes it may be helpful to divide people into small groups to pray, perhaps especially where there is something particular confronting the congregation. There are bound to be more formal occasions when these things are not appropriate but for a great deal of the time it will enrich worship when local and immediate concerns are held before God.

5 Valuing the Person

The ups and downs of life tend to be more visible in places characterized by a working class culture than will be so in middle class communities.

People can be more ready to celebrate and commiserate alongside one another. In areas of multiple deprivation there can also sometimes be a sub-current of unity in adversity. There is an open door for a church that also identifies with this.

One of the radical practices of the mid-Victorian Slum-Priest-Ritualists was to record the names of the otherwise forgotten departed around a 'Third Altar' in their churches. This was a way of saying that every person matters before God. In communities where life and death were cheap, and the role of funerals was to dispose of bodies rather than celebrate lives, this was a reminder of Christ's good news.

The stark inhumanity of the early inner city slums has gone from Britain but the connections for the church to make between people and God's love are still there to be made.

Occasional Offices

Funerals and weddings present vital opportunities for the church to join with people in holding the most significant things we encounter in our human existence before God. Among the Initiation rites, baptism also presents similar opportunities.

There can sometimes be a tension between the pastoral and missionary demands made by these occasions especially focused on the use of the sermon slot. For instance, it is all too easy for funerals to concentrate so much on the grief and loss of a loved person, and on all that has been good in their life, that the hope of the gospel is missed. There is danger in loading too much work on the sermon. An alternative and better way is to use the Gathering as a time to focus on the person whose life is being celebrated and whose death is being grieved over. This can be extensive and can easily involve members of the family and friends in spoken contributions, actions such as lighting an Easter Candle and in placing symbols or mementos around the coffin. The value of the person who is no longer with us is then the context for everything else that is said and done in the service. The sermon slot is free to be used as a reflection on the gospel and a faithful understanding of Christ.

In weddings it may also be possible to preface the service with the couples' story. All of the Initiation Rites, including baptism, suggest moments when testimony might be appropriate. In some traditions the notion of a testimony can be more than a little unwelcome. But this is not intended to be a particularly stylized contribution conforming to a foreign genre. Testimony is

Testimony is an invitation for an open and truly human story to be told of a local journey in faith

an invitation for an open and truly human story to be told of a local journey in faith. It should be natural and genuine. This is much more easily done where adults are being baptized or confirmed but most families bringing a child to the church for baptism will have their reasons. Why not listen to them and extend or extrapolate from them?

Personal Moments

Baptisms, weddings and funerals have deep roots connecting them with the church. Baby naming, civic marriage ceremonies and secular funerals are beginning to change this. But the traffic is not all one way. There are other moments in people's lives that some are increasingly wanting to celebrate before God:

- Birthdays
- Anniversaries
- Commemorations
- Blessing wedding ring
- Thanksgivings

In church these are often only short occasions including a prayer with some Bible reading and reflection. It may also be that some of the stories lying behind the occasion might be shared informally. Sometimes these moments can form part of another service, sometimes they might just involve a few people stood in a circle in the church's sanctuary, sometimes at home. But always they should mediate the love of God for those who come looking for his blessing and should direct their journey onwards along the path of faith.

Some churches are making creative use of the staged rites before and after funerals that are outlined in the *Common Worship: Pastoral Offices*.[9] Others use the service of Thanksgiving for the Gift of a Child from the same book as a staged rite prior to Baptism . These moments of prayer, dedication and reflection in the awareness of God's presence can have strong resonances in UPA contexts.

The Secular Calendar

There is a calendar outside the church that gives shape to the year and offers moments of celebration. Its high days are not without their resonances with Christian faith. And many people mark these dates in a serious way. It may be worth trying to build connections on them, although enthusiasm must be tempered with the recognition that these days are often already spoken for by rituals outside of the church. Making links with worship could be an uphill struggle.

- **New Year:** The religious calendar encourages services such as Commemoration of the Faithful Departed around All Saints' or All Souls' Days. It may be that there are better connections to be made for those whose lives do not revolve around the church at New Year. Recently departed loved ones are often missed most by their families and friends at Christmas time and New Year is a time of resolution and commitment to the future.

- **Valentine's Day:** *New Patterns for Worship* provides a sample service for Valentine's Day that draws on human love as a pointer to God's nature.[10] Consider using this as an annual occasion for the recently married to be invited back to church when they can thank God for their own love and be reminded of his.

- **Mothering Sunday and Fathers' Day:** In UPAs parents often receive a very bad press. Here is an opportunity to offer affirmation and pray over the responsibility of motherhood or fatherhood. They may provide an opportunity for recent baptism families to be invited back to church. On these occasions a restatement of the baptismal promises may be made. See also the ideas carried in the *New Patterns for Worship* sample services.[11]

Respecting the Corporate

6

Fellowship is a strong component of working class culture.

Where this is capitalized upon the church stands a better chance of growing into a communion of united disciples rather than the more common gathering of individual worshippers. A church of self-evident *koinonia* in turn can express the gospel well to a community that attaches high value to corporate identity.

The Project Church

One of the facets of communities where large numbers of people have been alienated from academic learning through cultural baggage and personal history is that personal development and growth are more likely to come through experiential learning rather than conceptual learning. The Project Church model has emerged as a new way of being church particularly in places where identity is conceived of primarily in corporate terms and where learning is primarily experiential.

'Projects' are well-defined activities in the church that provide a particular service to the local community. They may have paid staff but are run and managed primarily by volunteers most of whom will be rooted in the worshipping community. The church tends to encourage worshippers to see their discipleship as being expressed in engaging with such acts of service. And the volunteers grow in their sense of discipleship through working together and learning how to offer their service better. This is both practical and interpretive.[12]

The volunteers grow in their sense of discipleship through working together

Churches that consciously adopt this model may support a large number of projects. The projects themselves represent the mission of the church and should be established strategically. They may be constituted as a simple *ad hoc* group or they may become independent limited companies with charitable status. There may be local people of generous spirit who are not otherwise a part of the church who want to give time to these as good causes. Undoubtedly, it will largely be members of the worshipping community, inspired by God and longing to see the kingdom come, who are most likely to take a lead. The 'projects' become a very significant ragged edge in their churches.

These projects can have a huge knock-on effect towards the way that worship connects with the lives of the church's members. Churches that do not adopt the model wholeheartedly are still also likely to have branches and satellite groups that have similar connections and offer opportunities for prayer and worship.

Celebrating the Small: Apt Liturgies

Projects that are connected to the church can grow to see that relationship as a bind. When the church has been the parent of a project it may be inevitable that there will be a period of rebellion sooner or later. It is really important that projects are encouraged to appreciate the faith that inspired the work and the spiritual dimension that faith adds. The church should not just be about sponsoring charitable work but it is about responding to the will of God for a more heavenly world. Calling those involved in projects to prayer and worship provides an important reminder of the faith that gave rise to the original vision. Such groups will have their own celebrations and failures. They will have their comings and goings, their anniversaries and their griefs. All of this should be anchored in prayer and worship, not such that it dominates their life but enough that it beckons project members onwards to the source of all inspiration. This can include:

- A Prayer before an outing;
- A start of year or start of term service;
- Commemoration after a death;
- Farewell to those moving on.

Using Seasons, Especially Christmas

At Christmas time a small urban church surrounded by a range of project work can start to feel like a cathedral as worship leaders have more Carol Services to organize than there are days in December. And even such traditional worship can break new ground for people who can be encouraged to connect faith with the activity that has drawn them to look to the church. For young members of a Parent and Toddler Group taking part in a nativity it can be the first time they have ever been in church and drawn into a gospel message.

Some groups may respond particularly well to a harvest thanksgiving, such as line dancers, whose country dancing makes strong harvest connections, and lunch clubs that gather in many churches to enjoy a meal.

What Has God Been Doing?

It is important to keep the worshipping community that gathers Sunday-by-Sunday abreast of all that is done in their name. Those who contribute to a church's project life can also witness powerfully to the way that God is leading them on if they are given the chance. Regular opportunities in the context of Sunday worship to ask what God has been doing in some of the church's weekday work can be a way of capitalizing on this. That can be done as part of the Sermon or before the Intercessions or the Peace quite easily.

Children's Groups

Children's groups can also mirror the pattern of an adult church given to supporting a range of satellite projects and being enriched by that work. Where there is diverse provision for children and young people throughout the week this can be drawn together and brought into worship on a Sunday in a way that is not necessarily constrained by the needs of adults. So members of a Boys' Brigade or Brownies or a youth club can be invited to join together for worship as well as attendance at their groups' meetings.

Children's groups might well be characterized more by worship than the learning focus that Sunday Schools have

Sunday children's groups might well have their meeting time characterized more by worship than the learning focus that traditional Sunday Schools often have. This might well follow the structure of *A Service of the Word* and draw on resources such as those in *New Patterns for Worship*. This can provide a context for exploring the faith as well as providing a place where stories from the weekday groups can be shared, but primarily it is about drawing youngsters into a sense of the presence of God. It ought also to integrate in some way with the adult church. When adults and children join together it can easily feel to the children as if they are going to be confined by what adults do. Children should be given the opportunity to play back to the adults something from their own session.

Parades

Not every youngster that takes part in a church's weekday activities is going to be ready to attend worship every week. Occasional all-age services and church parades pitched particularly at these groups can be a way of focussing their commitment enough to gather a much wider group. Parades, with the opportunity to carry a group's colours, connect very well with the style of some uniformed organizations. It may be that non-uniformed organizations can be encouraged to contribute to the worship in other ways such as drama, music or dance. Youth club members probably know the current pop scene better than anybody else in your church. How about getting them to suggest a pop song that can be played to the congregation each time with a little statement about what it might say to the church?

Church and Establishment

One of the lessons of the Slum-Priest-Ritualists, hinted at in Chapter 1, is that their gospel appeal to the urban poor amongst whom they ministered was probably very much wrapped up in their oppression by the British establishment. Where church parades are developed into Civic Services or formal Remembrance Services it is important to ask who the church is identifying with. The way that honoured dignitaries can bring significance to worship in a middle class community might not work in quite the same way in some UPAs. Such services are possible and sometimes even important. But it is vital that the church does not glorify powerful people. Rather it must help them identify with its struggle for peace and justice and help them worship God who offers us glimpses of heaven no matter where we live.

The church must help the community worship God who offers us glimpses of heaven no matter where we live

A God of Forgiveness or a God of Hope

7

When living in a poor urban community it quickly becomes apparent that many individuals have very low self-esteem.

This is compounded by a community self-image derived from the stories the local and national media carry about life there—anti-social behaviour, crime, unemployment, poor housing and underachievement. It may be true that it is difficult to know the forgiveness of God until you are aware of your own need for forgiveness. It may be that in comfortable parts of the world people need to be reminded of their own sin every time they seek to bring themselves together to worship God. However, the starting point is surely different in communities characterized by multiple deprivation.

One of the strengths of the evangelical tradition has been an ability to bring people to a sense of conviction of their own sin and so to realize the magnitude of God's love and forgiveness. Much liturgy works in the same way. *Common Worship* services almost universally conform to a normative structure in which confession and absolution are part of The Gathering. Whilst this is a strength in some cultural contexts, it may be a weakness in others.

Why should not worship sometimes begin with the people of God being built up, reminded that God has chosen them, directed to reflect on the blessings of the past week and the temptations that they have not given into? Why must it always be the sins—sins that the oppressive forces of the world do not allow people in UPAs to forget—that also need to greet their entry into the conscious presence of God? Of course it is perfectly legal for Anglican worship to begin in more positive and uplifting ways. It just is not very common.

The starting point may be to discover him firstly as a God of hope rather than forgiveness

In a similar vein, it is quite permissible to place prayers of penitence after the Liturgy of the Word in services such as Holy Communion Order One. But this can hardly be said to be encouraged. There is no rubric contained in the service itself, only a note 148 pages after the rite's last page. This apparent need for minimum deviation from a dominant order for Communion betrays assumptions about the uniformity of

British culture, and the starting points that people have as they gather before God, that will not enhance our mission in many places. Of course, A Service of the Word allows limitless changes to this but it is most likely going to be Holy Communion Order One that will shape the mindset of the church to the greatest extent in the coming years.

This liturgical challenge is also a challenge to the mission of the church. The starting point for people whose lives are spent under oppressive conditions may be to discover him firstly as a God of hope rather than forgiveness. It is instructive to see how the people of Jesus' day encountered him. Whilst the rich and powerful were challenged to repentance, the poor and marginalized first encounter him as a harbinger of hope and healing. For instance, the rich young man was asked to go and give all he had to the poor; the poor were told they were blessed for the kingdom of heaven was theirs. The church's mission and liturgy might do well to reflect this truth.

Notes

1   *Faith in the City: Report of the Archbishop of Canterbury's Commission on Urban Priority Areas* (Church Information Office: London, 1985).

2   *Our Towns and Cities: The Future—Delivering Urban Renaissance. Urban White Paper Executive Summary*, Rt Hon John Prescott, Deputy Prime Minister (DETR, London: 2000).

3   *Church and People in an Industrial City*, E R Wickham (Lutterworth Press, London: 1957).

4   *Census of Great Britain, 1851: Religious Worship, England and Wales. Report and Tables. Presented to Both Houses of Parliament by Command of Her Majesty* , Horace Mann (HMSO / Eyre and Spottiswoode: London, 1853) p 93.

5   For example B Bernstein, 'Education cannot compensate for society' in B Cosin *et al, School and Society* (Routledge and Kegan Paul: London, 1971).

6   My *Interactive Preaching* (Grove Worship booklet W 144) is an attempt to discuss this model more fully.

7   These teams were originally called *Groups for Urban Ministry and Leadership (GUML).* They were attractive even in non-UPA parishes and a whole diocese scheme called SMT (Shared Ministry Teams) has now been established. These teams train first to operate as a group and exercise leadership. It is only as they become able to do this that they secondly begin to explore what their ministries might be.

8   Roland and Kevin Mayhew each respectively provide the necessary hardware and software.

9   *Common Worship: Pastoral Offices* (Church House Publishing: London, 2001).

10 *New Patterns for Worship* (Church House Publishing: London, 2002) Sample Service 13.

11 *New Patterns for Worship* Sample Services 14 and 15.

12 Ann Morisy has written this model up in her important book, *Beyond the Good Samaritan* (DLT: London, 1997).